HOPEFUL

THOUGHTS

FEARFUL

DREAMS

P. J. LUMSDEN

Acknowledgement

With great thanks to my brother, Colin Lumsden,
without who's help I would not have been able to
publish my work....Thank you Brother..

WHERE HAS LIFE GONE

I look at my life as it passes me by,
And often I start to wonder why.
Why I have done the things that I've done,
And why I have not the things I have sought.
I wanted a good life I wanted some fun,
Was it to much to ask for a life in the sun.

True I must say I've been blessed with much good,
I just cannot remember tho' I know that I should.
There's times I've had fun and lay in the sun,
But they've been hidden by dark clouds one after one.
My future seems lost in a vast emptiness,
But reaching it's end never the less.

My mind has been lost in the shadowy mists of time,
And I cannot seem to get back on lifes line.
I smoke and I drink I work and I sleep,
But now lifes gradient seems to be getting so steep.
The fun that I had when I was only a lad,
Seems to have left me forever,
And I wonder if ever again I'll be glad.

LEAVE ME ALONE

What do I think what do I see,
What are my thoughts on reality.
Do I see truth do I see lies,
What do you see deep in my eyes.
Can you see love can you see hate,
Do you think I have hope or is it to late.

What are my views on every day news,
Would you not care to stand in my shoes.

My thoughts are my own I see what I see,
I make up my own reality.
The truth that I know are lies gone before,
And you can see nothing behind my closed door.
What future in love what future in hope,
I'd rather get wrecked on illegal dope.

What are my views I think you now know,
They mean nothing to you so leave me alone.

THE SNIPER

He watches out from his place of hiding,
That lonely man they call the sniper.
He watches out with cold dark eyes,
And picks and chooses when gun he fires.
He hides in trees and underground,
Just happy knowing he'll not be found.

He picks of men and widows wives,
And when out of bullets he'll use his knives.
He does not care who does fall,
They're all the same both one and all.
He's not alone this man the sniper,
For underground or in a tree,
There is another who's his enemy.

NOT FOR MAN

Crystal skies of setting sun,
World of magic man does shun.
Books he reads of yesteryears,
He finds them fun and sheds no tears.
Reality is what man see's
And destroys the forest of magic trees.

But wizards watch from far away,
And again one day shall have their say.
And man shall cower, full of fear,
At last he'll shed the magic tear.
He'll watch the wizards casting spells,
With sounds of magic tolling bells.

And man shall learn to be more kind,
And listen to old nature's mind.
Mistakes he's make shall be his last,
As final spells the wizards cast.
And now the earth once more be free,
A magic world we will not see.

A SUMMERS DOOR

With melting snow the spring does come,
Awaiting rays of a summers sun.
And colour once again does strive,
As mother nature comes alive.

The bitter chill of a winters wind,
Departs once more to let the sunshine in.
And rainbows fill a freshened sky,
While cold dark nights begin to fly.

Mountain streams begin to seep,
Out from a long and cold dark sleep.
And flowers spring from earths green floor,
As nature opens her summers door

A SCOTTISH EMPIRE

Scotland the brave Scotland the true,
Once she was free for me and for you.
Then after war and battle galore,
She was stolen by England to be ours no more.

They say we are part of a british empire,
But our souls are aflame with Scottish fire.
They give us their laws and tell us obey,
I wait for our freedom I long for that day.

Our oil from our shores and blood from our veins,
Are taken away for englands own gains.
The kilts and the daggers from father to son,
Shall once more pass downwards and Scotland be one.

How long will it take how long will it be,
Until once more Scotland will fight to be free.
When will they surrender when will they all tire,
And leave us at peace,
With our Scottish empire.

MY FRIEND

My friend, cause that is what you are,
In times of trouble I'm never far.
So do not fear to call on me,
If my views you want to see.

Through out the years we have been close,
Held together by some hidden force.
Tho' we may part in years to come,
My hope is that we stay as one.

And when we are old and our time nears,
We'll remember back to younger years.
And thou' through time our thoughts may alter,
I pray our friendship will never falter.

So come my friend we'll drink some beer,
And raise our glass to lifes own cheer.
But thou' the years may for us be cruel,
Let friendship be our only rule.

FREE WORLD

Kill, destroy, murder, maim,
Insanity of your brain.
Thoughts of evil blinding lust,
All men's souls turn into dust.
Evil thoughts within ones mind,
Disastrous future of mankind.

Blackened thoughts within your head,
All mankind one day be dead.
Destruction of the world we live in,
All our souls corrupt with sin.
Fighting onward to our end,
Will mans thinking never end.

Destroying nations one by one,
Beneath the eye of natures sun.
The evil on this planet be,
The human element that's you and me.
But one day soon our time will come,
And the earth no longer belong to man.

FOR THE JACOBITE

Our flag shall stand upon a land,
A land again that's free.
Our hills shall sing the highland songs,
Again for you and me.
Our people will again become,
The governers of great Scotland.

The spirit of our fathers be,
Triumphant in our new glory.
And highland clans again be true,
To highland hearts and me and you.
And parliament shall be no more,
In governing the Scottish shore.

So just remember always,
The freedom that we seek.
And for the Jacobite,
Vengeance we shall wreak.
And once again we'll raise the flag,
Upon the land of free Scotland.

OUR SCOTLAND

In 1745 we fought to stay alive,
And on our hills and glens,
We drew our bloody knives.
And then the clans from near and far,
Joined up to fight as one.
Against invading forces of neighbouring England.

We fought at Killiekrankie,
And won at English cost,
But at Culloden Moor,
Our righteous cause was lost.
But freedom is our future,
And freedom is our right.
And one day soon we'll show them,
The strength of Scottish might.

The right to run our country,
Shall be ours again some day.
And after we have risen,
No more shall England have her say.
Now the future of our country,
Is up to you and me,
And if we stand together always,
Then always we'll be free.

GLORY TO KNOW

A northern flower on a distant shore,
Fighting for freedom nothing more.
A country of people who want to be free,
After all it's our right cant you see.
The country that tells us what we are to do,
Means nothing to me and nothing to you.

The country that holds us is hungry for power,
But we shall defeat them when times comes our hour.
A country we've fought for hundreds of years,
We shall destroy without any tears.
Great men have fought for us through all history,
But now for the future the warriors are we.

This country for freedom, this country so proud,
I shout out the name I shout it out loud.
All shout for great Scotland, Scotland so true,
One day she'll be free for me and for you.
Down with old England down she must go,
And Scotland shall rise and glory to know.

CHILDREN OF THE GLENS

Music flows,
Down from the glens.
The sound,
Of piping highland men.
And tunes,
Of glory shall we sing.
And sounds,
Of Scottish freedom bring.
We'll march,
Upon the southern land.
And free,
Our noble great Scotland.
No more,
To bow to English lords.
We'll cut,
Forever all southern cords.

The Scottish,
Flag once more be proud.
With shaking,
Off the English shroud.
And Scottish,
Lands be free once more.
And Scotland,
Govern her own shore.
The Celtic,
Clans of the northern land.
Will stand,
Together hand in hand.
And future,
Children of the glens.
Will live,
In freedom with Celtic friends.

THE FINAL DAY

A move in chess a chance of life,
It's all a game to me.
Reality is not real its all just fantasy.
Our lives are used for bargaining,
Between the super powers.
Destruction of our planet,
With radiation showers.

All life will cease one day to live,
Upon this planet earth.
The game of chance has now become,
A nightmare of the truth.
And man will end his terror reign,
No more to deal out senseless pain.

We live each day on borrowed time,
Awaiting for the fire.
The world a blackened wilderness,
A planet funeral pyre.
And all the knowledge that we have sought,
Will be lost within a hidden thought.

And the universe will carry on,
Without a thought for us.
It will create another race,
To fill the human place.
So lets just hope that they,
Will never see the final day.

TUNES OF WAR

One thousand pipers massed the hill,
With hearts on fire they wait to kill.
To end the lives of southern men,
And free for always their thistled glen.

All pipes call out for fighting men,
To search their hearts and fight again.
And help our land to come alive,
And seek vengeance for the 45.

The Scottish flag again to fly,
On Scottish land neath Scottish sky.
And highland winds being to blow,
As piping men play tunes of war.

A fighting force that will not die,
Begin to march with the freedom cry.
And men from southern lands will fall,
And Scotland will again stand tall.

The blood we shed out from our veins,
Will be worth the freedom that Scotland gains.
No more to bow to English laws,
For Scotland hath regained her cause.

FOREVER BE

Forest hill and mountain glen,
Cry out to all your highland men.
So they may rise and fight for you,
And send the English south again.
Cry for men to free your lands,
From beneath the clutches of southern hands.

Oh' brook and burn and thistle flower,
Give us strength for our glory hour.
Let the pipes sing out again,
And free us from the English reign.
All men of Scotland arise to arms,
So Scotland can regain her charms.

The Scottish hills shall come alive,
And highland hearts again to strive.
To free our lands for Scotsmen true,
Forever free both me and you.
So children of the north unite,
And help the land of Scotland fight.

We will be free again some day,
And send old England on her way.
Destruction of an age old foe,
Forever southwards they shall go.
And Scotland once again be free,
Free forever and forever be.

WHAT FUTURE

A future world of darkness,
Whose colour it has gone.
A future without feeling,
The heat of summers sun.
A future where all life,
Will live beneath the ground,
A future world of silence,
Without the love of nature's sound.

A future world of sadness,
When family life is lost.
A future without loved ones,
On a world of burning frost.
A future that's created,
From within the minds of men.
A future world of emptiness,
Disaster without end.

A future world of man's creation,
A planet wilderness.
A future without caring,
For love or happiness.
A future place in time,
Without reason without rhyme.
A future without fun,
That future has begun.

MANS BLINDNESS

Death and destruction,
The legacy of man.
A world made of confusion,
What right have we to be.

Destruction of environment,
A world thats full of hate.
A planet in the wilderness,
Of a never ending space.

A world made of pollution,
From within the minds of men.
An ocean full of darkness,
Life's bitter fatal end.

Red and green and black and grey,
The end of life to come someday.
A whisky in the hands of men,
Makes mind intent on destruction.

Friends to find and friends depart,
To make you glad or break your heart.
A hope for the future of mankind,
I hope one day we'll stop being blind.

WORLD OF MAGIC

Magic skies,
Of purple haze.
Watch upon,
The wizards gaze.
Warlocks, witches.
Elfs and gnomes.
Bringing magic,
Inside your homes.
Mountain peaks,
That touch the sky.
Hold old wise men,
Who never die.

Fairies dance,
Round elfen fires.
As wizards watch,
The hidden shires.
Lords and heros,
Ride the land.
Searching for,
A maidens hand.
Dragons fly,
In coloured sky.
World of magic,
Never die.

FUTURE TIMES

The wind does howl
And scream in night.
While hoards of demons
On wing take flight.
Old witches laugh,
While casting spells.
As man lies hidden,
From tolling bells.
Old wizards walk,
The mountain pass.
In search of truth,
From times long past.
A thought that lies,

While time stands still.
Will awaken with,
A burning chill.
And future generations fight,
A war of thoughts,
That they think right.
And after man destroys his home,
The demons and dragons again
shall roam.
And the world will pass into hands,
Of elfen lords to rule the land.

ALL SOLDIERS CRY

A war is fought by common man,
For governments of his land.
For kings and queens and crazed dictators,
Who hide behind their safety shelters.

And man is sent to fight a foe,
To fight a foe he does not know.
And thousands die to gain some land,
To give his leaders the upper hand.

Wives are left to cry alone,
The desecration of their home.
And children grow not knowing why,
Why their fathers had to die.

While safe at home the leaders speak,
And send the soldier to his darkened sleep.
And no one ever questions why,
After war all soldiers cry.

MIND DEATH

Disaster strikes from within my soul,
Searching for my inner goal.
Thoughts of madness flood my head,
As I walk the streets of the living dead.
What see you within mine eye,
Can you see your time to die.
Walk with me within the shadows,
Do not fear the blood red meadows.
Play with thoughts that aren't your own,
And be forever all alone.
Don't let my thoughts within your mind,
For your brain will become blind.

Be you live or be you dead,
Keep your thoughts outside my head.
Questions that have got no answers,
Creep upon you as death advances.
Dark black shapes that somehow glow,
From within your mind do flow.
Listen to the screams of night,
As all the devils horeds take flight.
Now your feelings deep within,
Inside your head they start to spin,
And now your future upon the earth,
Will now forever have no worth.

COMMON MAN

I came upon a murder, and wondered what to do,
I asked him why he did it, and he said what's it to you.
I couldn't find an answer, so turned to walk away,
Then he said well won't you listen to what I have to say.

I'm just a common man, who's trying to find a job,
This man he has got millions, but me he tried to rob.
To rob me of my soul, and make me be his slave,
But I am tired of people, to whom my money gave.

They treat me like a nothing, and send me to my grave,
Without a single penny,
when to the world my life I gave.
And I thought I can relate, to what this man he says,
So I shook his hand and walked away,
From beneath this killers gaze.

WORLD WAR

It took one power crazy fool,
To plunge the world to war.
But it took the lives of millions,
To stop what he stood for.
And after battle in the killing fields,
A soldier stands alone,
His comrades lie beside his feet,
As dead as his enemy.
And he bows his head and wonders why,
So many good men had to die.

And after years of fighting,
He returns to his own shore.
The war it now is over,
And with memories must he live.
With thoughts that are sometimes hazy,
Of a world that once went crazy.
And even now in his twilight years,
The faces of his friends he sees.
As they lie upon the ground,
With open mouths that make no sound.

EVILS WAR

Shadows hide within the night,
The blackened shapes of evils fight.
The forces of the beast unseen,
Will fight the fight with hands unclean.

To kill and torture scare and maim,
And drive all men to think insane.
The evil wings of Satan's lair,
Will drive all men to think despair.

The blackened shroud of deaths grim reaper,
Does send mens souls to hell and deeper.
And far beneath the earths weak crust,
Man's soul begins to die from lust.

The light does fade as time goes by,
And darkness comes by evils cry.
The war will always be this way,
The fight between both night and day.

REALITY

Reality is what you know it to be,
But who can say what others see.
Our minds are different both one and all,
Only you yourself can see beyond the wall.
Our minds they think of what they know,
Within our minds our own thoughts glow.
And what I see with these eyes of mine,
May not exactly tow your thoughts line.

My images of sight and thought,
Are mine alone and cannot be caught.
You see what I see just as well,
But what images arise on your mind cell.
I see the day and I see the night,
But my mind still waits to see the light.
I see reality as I know it to be,
But who can say what reality others see.

REVERSE THOUGHT

Thought transfer, transfer thought,
Mind speech, speak your mind.
Think power, power of thought,
Brain matter, matter of fact.
Eyes see, see through eyes,
Mind thinks, think through mind.

Power struggle, struggle for power,
Want war, war on want.
Never fear, fear forever,
Shooting star, star struck.
Reverse thought, thought reversal,
Work wanted, wanting work.

Plant seed, seedling plant,
Near or far, far or near.
Running faster, standing still,
Flying over, crawling under.
Never think, thought of always,
Blue sky cannot see.

END OF EVOLUTION

A million miles through time and space,
A million years to create a race.
But that race was evil that race was ill,
In no time at all it learnt to kill.
Forever wanting when most are in need,
What a failure of time this was indeed.

Now two thousand years have come and gone,
And man has created the nuclear bomb.
As people are starving both young and old,
The earth is caught in a fatal hold.
Now man can destroy at the touch of a button,
What nature created with the first explosion.

Now millions of years of time and space,
Will be destroyed by this mad race.
In just a few disastrous seconds,
Man will have fired the fatal weapons.
And man will never be no more,
For man has fought his final war.

WAR CHILD

He was born in a storm in "45",

No one thought that he'd survive.

Born on a star so far away,

He came here to earth he came here to stay.

He's fought many battles through the years,

And never once has he shed tears.

His eyes were red and his hair was fair,

And he tore through the world without a care.

Then came the day that everybody dread,

And the ones that survived would wish they were dead.

Because power had gone to the war childs head.

Now the war child sits in his shelter so brave,

And he sends all of us to live in our grave.

And now the skies are alive with giant mushrooms,

Like devilish brides with devilish grooms.

And one day soon he'll pay for his crimes,

They'll send him to hell to work Satans mines.

He was born in a storm in "45",

And no one thought that he'd survive.

But his final battle he lost and it cost,

For the war child started a nuclear holocaust.

PAST FUTURE

Gone, gone for all time,

The richness of land that was once yours and mine.

Those mystical times of witches and elfs,

Of warlocks and fairies and magic on shelves

Heroes that were and heroes that are,

Are two sorts of people so near yet so far.

Those mystical times when dragons fought kings,

Those magical songs that brought death with their stings.

When maidens were helped by knights on white steeds,

And black witches were beaten by peoples own needs.

Those magical times of days long ago,

Are lost to us now for all evermore.

MEMORIES

Rewind your thoughts to times gone by,
Think a thought into the sky.
Pass through life without a care,
And raise your glass to life's own cheer.

Remind yourself of younger years,
When you had fun and shed few tears.
When all your friends had, thoughts as yours,
And you danced along life's long wide shores.

But now these years they start to fly,
And very soon you're going to die.
The views of friends have come and gone,
And when friends depart you'll be alone
With memories.

TIME TO END

Little worlds collided in an atmosphere,
Thats not too far from here,
In another dimension.
There are people in another galaxy,
Will they always be,
Or like you and me will they also die.

Time is very old my friend,
Where did it begin,
Do you think it will ever end,
Infinity.
Can't you see it will always be,
Until worlds collide in an atmosphere,
That is really here.

And the sun explodes and you will die,
And time will end my friend,
Who cares why.
All that we have done,
And all that's to come,
Will be lost forever in the endless emptiness,
Of a voidless sun.

MY SOUL TO BE FREE

My soul will fly it will not die,
From my body that is bound by earth.
Into natures arms and gods own charms,
My soul will hold its own worth.
My soul will soar my goal to score,
And my sins to be washed clean away.

My body's held by earths tight grip,
But my spirit has started its trip.
The visions of dreams I've had through the years,
Are now reality seen through deaths dark tears.
Freedom has come with lifes last breath,
And all evil is left far behind on cold earth.

Into the kingdom of beauty and love,
Forever to wander at peace.
To live now forever inside the rays of the sun,
And forever be free of life's leash.
To wander the heavens for time evermore.
My soul to be free my spirit to soar.

TIME TO CHANGE

Straight between the eyes,
The arrow flies.
Truth is hard to bear,
Said without care.
The tears are never dried,
When hurt inside.
And life it must go on,
When feelings gone.

You live from day to day,
But never say.
The thoughts that are inside,
Are hard to hide.
Your thoughts they are your own,
When your alone.
And always wonder why,
It's hard to cry.

You sit inside your room,
Full of gloom.
And as the years pass by,
You wonder why.
And now you start to wonder,
The stress your under,
And now your plans to leave,
You start to weave.

UNIVERSAL WIZARDRY

Wizards of the universe,
Watch down upon mankind.
To see what they created,
From within each others mind.
Ancient figures give a silent cry,
From a time that's long past by.
And as they watch each other,
They begin to wonder why.
Why a world which they created,
Turned out to be so cruel.
And why as time passed by,
Man grew up to be a fool.

Now the future of mankind,
Will be studied from above.
From the eyes of watching wizards,
Who created life from love.
And the raven shall descend,
When now the world one day will end.
And mighty spells from wizards cast,
Until man be dead at last.
Then the world shall carry on,
And the world shall live as one.
Until time its time has come,
And in universe the world be none.

TIMES MIST

The flames of desire,
Grow higher and higher.
Inside the souls of men.
The spirit that is aching,
And crying for freedom,
Will never be captured again.

A black emptiness,
An expanse of everness,
And a spirit set to fly.
While deep within yourself,
You hear the never ending cry,
Of a soul that will not die.

And light from the black,
Is traveling back,
Trying to capture your eye.
But you cannot see,
Your own reality,
And are lost in times mist evermore.

THOUGHTS

Stranger of the light,
A stalker in the night.
Pawn in Satan's hand,
A waster of the land.
Killer without thought,
His victims will be taught.
Your future in his hands,
A grave beneath the sands.

Barer of the word,
His knowledge must be heard.
A search with second sight,
From a monumental height.
A burning flame within.
The cavern of our sin.
A soul that must depart,
From the spirit of the heart.

A thought that echoes from,
A distant freedom song.
A way that must be sought,
Is what the teacher taught.
A generation gap,
Hides secrets in its trap.
And knowledge it must be,
The freedom we decree.

MOUNTAIN

Rising high up into the heavens,

Majestically supreme in its awesome power.

Snow capped mighty and strong.

Silent and as still as the night,

Until challenged by man.

Beginning from lowly beginnings,

And rising on up to the sun.

Through forests and valleys and glens,

Through rivers and torrents of fire.

Surrounded by lochs lakes and seas.

Forever by sight never moving,

But never a day it stands still.

Battered by hail rain sleet and snow,

Onwards forever upwards does go.

Into the clouds it reaches on up to the sky.

Thou' man sometimes reaches the summit,

He'll never conquer its power.

For its power is life and is death,

For God created the mountain,

And the mountain created the man.

DARK MINDS

Minds that are fighting, minds that are waring,
Minds that are forever never at peace.
Thoughts that are hazy, see through eyes that are crazy
And all deeds are done without thought.
Thoughts that are black, insanely evil,
Visions of death and destruction.
The psycho he sits, alone in the shadows,
Awaiting the coming of victims.

Destruction of land, with axe in his hand,
Insanely awaiting the kill.
His mind is aflame, all thoughts are insane,
And his anger is hungry for flesh.
With blood in his eyes, his thoughts in disguise,
He stealthily walks the night street.
His killings begin, as victims he meets,
And life is exchanged for mad lust.

DEATH OF CREATION

He said, let there be light,
And light there was.
He said, let there be life,
and life began.
He said, let there be thought,
And a quest was sought.

Now man had the glory,
But He wanted the power.
His mind kept creating,
And creation meant death.
He blinded the people,
But they were easily lead.

He looked to the night sky,
And watching the stars.
He built himself spaceships,
And visited Mars.
But on his return trip,
When he was alone.
He noticed that man,
Had destroyed his own home.

TIME

Never ending, never dying,
Always over not begun.
Always laughing, always crying,
Forever sad but full of fun.

Distant voices from the future,
Distant voices from the past.
Images of peace images of war.
Images of death when newly born.

Minds that are peaceful, minds that are sad,
Minds that are wanting, thoughts that have had.
Memories of good times, thoughts of the bad,
Remembrance of laughter some never had.

Tears that have fallen, and those yet to fall,
Smile at the future or at the past.
Cry for tomorrow today never lasts.
When at last you are taken,
Can you be sure where you'll go.

RELIGION OF GOD

Kneel by the great cross your soul is on fire,
Pray with your clasped hands from down deep within.
Speaking with God don't be a liar,
Tell Him the truth your deep heartfelt sin.

Does He listen I wonder I cannot tell,
Do you think He'll forgive or send you to hell.
Do you dare wonder if He really does care.
Or do you secretly hope He's really not there.

When you have told Him that you are sad,
Do you think He'll be happy angry or glad.
And if after finally you do not repent,
Do you not wonder where your next life is spent.

EARTH LIGHT

From darkness the light it does travel,
From out of beyond of the skies.
You can see it at night as it sparkles,
Through blackness and time and beyond.

Somewhere far out in that dark night sky,
Are minds that think just as we do.
Somewhere far out in that deep blackness,
Someone watches a light that is you.

Over distance of billions of light years,
The thoughts of their minds are as one.
Is there life their all thinking,
On that planet that's third from the sun.

THOUGHTFUL STREAMS

Castle walls of crystal blue,
Flames within the heartbeat true.
Thoughts and feelings from the past,
Held in memories to ever last.

Truth within the mind does flow,
Inside your heart your feelings grow.
Desire for another time,
In a world of magic golden rhyme.

Fires burn in elfen dreams,
Fairies dance round mountain streams.
Wizards talk of stories old,
When they were young and all were bold.

Eyes that see inside of sight,
Are held within the minds of right.
Old wise men who never falter,
Pray beside the ancient altar.

Dreams of flaming setting suns,
In magic skies the comet runs.
Bright red dawns of burning fire,
Etched within the funeral pyre.

While pixie lords ride the land,
Their world is held by magic hand.
Their lives are held within your dreams,
Inside of flowing thoughtful streams.

THE DINOSAUR

For 150 million years they ruled,
The dragons of the plains.
Colossal creatures on the wing,
And Tyrannosaurus Rex's.

Inside a world of giant trees,
The dinosaurs they roamed.
Hunting down each other,
In their never ending war.

But disaster struck their harmony,
And their end was near at hand.
For extinction was their only end,
No more to walk the land.

DRAGON KINGS

Giant lords of long ago,
Masters of an age.
In times great book,
Their reign was short,
Nothing but a page.

Rulers of the planet earth,
A kingdom full of power.
But their time was short in history,
Nothing but an hour.

For nine score million years they walked
Upon a new born world.
But time did pass,
And they did die lost in mystery.

Now nothing but their bones remain,
Lying buried in the ground.
And no one knows for sure the things,
That destroyed the reign
Of dragon kings.

CREATIONS EYE

A speck of dust,
In the eye of time.
A blue green planet,
That's yours and mine.
A void of time,
Without an end.
An expanse of emptiness.

A million suns surrounded,
By a million suns and more.
A galaxy of galaxy's,
Inside of nature's door.
A starry sky that wanders,
On forever more.

A never ending universe,
In a never ending sky.
A starry velvet ebony,
Inside of natures eye.
A glowing mass of energy,
That will never ever die,
This is nature's finest,
Inside creations eye.

FINAL JOURNEY

A bridge of time,
That spans through life.
A thought of hope,
Or assassin's knife.
You have to choose,
Which road to take.
There are so many,
In this world of fate.

A world of dark,
A world of light.
A silent thought,
From second sight.
Which road to take,
Which road to choose.
You must choose wisely,
Or life to lose.

A silent wish,
For what may be,
A hidden cry,
For reality.
These are the thoughts,
We sometimes crave.
Before our journey,
Into the grave.

LISTEN TO THE PEOPLE

Listen to the people,
To what the people say.
We vote you into power,
And we can help you stay.
But if you tell us lies,
Then the people shall despise.
And if to us you close your ears,
Then the time has come,
For blood and tears.

If the people of this world unite,
To fight against the fools.
Who govern over nations,
With idiotic rules.
Then truth and justice shall prevail,
And the souls of life,
Will be no longer up for sale.

So just listen to the people,
To what the people say.
Just listen to our thoughts and fears,
And there will be no cause for blood and tears.
Don't govern us with stupid rules,
And no longer will we think you fools.
Just listen to the people,
To what the people say.

TO MY LOVE

The flame of love
Is once again rekindled,
Inside my lonely heart.
My hopes and dreams
Again rejoice
The opening of my inner voice.

I lie alone awake at night,
With just your vision in my eye.
My thoughts they think
Of none but you
And my heart begins to cry.

I have no words to tell you,
The feelings in my heart.
Oh' if only you could see,
Those feelings in my eyes.
For once too often I have been hurt,
And fear to free my heart.

LIFE DREAM

I had a dream,
That I dreamt about a dream.
And then awoke to find,
It was reality.
I closed my eyes once again,
But sleep it would not come.

A future spent within a dream,
That turned out to be nightmarish.
And hidden thoughts,
Within my head
Of a sleep that would not finish.

I walk through life,
Each passing day.
But I can never escape,
Life's reality.
The thoughts that I think,
Are dreams that I dream.
And nothing is ever,
What you hope it to be.

FOREVER FREE

The north will rise from the ashes of death,

And free us from the English wreath.

The rebellion of the 45 will once more come alive.

The kilted clans of our domain,

Will once more forever, live again.

Our hills and glens will be our own,

And England shall have to walk alone.

The future plans of you and me,

To see our children are born free.

The future of our Scotland be,

For you and I forever free.

A SUPER HUMAN RACE?

A volcanic world created,
With a new born universe.
A billion years of cooling,
Then creation of a race.

An oasis in the ocean,
Of a starry ebony.
A planet full of plenty,
Until greed it was conceived.

A plant always wanting more,
Kept reaping from the land.
With not a single thought,
For the future of their kind.

And then one day they learnt to kill,
From there was no return.
And murder was the legacy,
Of a so called super race.

THE PHOENIX BIRD

Hidden thoughts lie undisturbed,
Inside the wings,
Of the phoenix bird.
Arising from the heart of fire,
Is this the creature of desire.

A magic death to come alive,
For this magic mystic bird.
With flaming wings it is reborn,
But its cry is never heard.

She cries in silent ecstasy,
As her life begins to soar.
Arising from the ashes,
To live again once more.

The flaming wings begin to rise,
Into the sky she once more flies.
A joyous feeling deep inside,
As she sings her new born song.

And she shall fly the clear blue sky,
And never come to harm.
She'll rise above the heavens,
With just her gracefulness and charms.

So come my friends and just take heed,
Of what this bird she does.
When she rises from the ashes,
And can still retain her love.

DEATHS PARADISE

Where are you going in life,
Thoughts flying past on the wind.
Years of hard work are taking their toll,
And you always seem deeper in debt.

Nothing goes right in your life anymore,
Everything seems to backfire.
Retirement seems to get nearer each day,
And happiness just out of reach.

Your anger builds up but still you don't speak,
And resentment is hidden away.
You live by a code implanted through time,
And in silence you enter your grave.

Now peace has come at last my friend,
Happiness for time evermore.
For not all have forgotten your goodness,
And repayment is mine says the Lord.

MY BROKEN HEART

You broke my heart my lost sweet lass,
And my love still feels the pain.
Thou' many years have wandered by,
My love still loves in vain.

I do not think my heart will heal,
The break I fear to great.
And now I fear again to love,
Without your love to feel.

I pray one day we will again,
Be joined our hearts together.
For even in my dreams I know,
There will never be another.

The dreams I dream are still of you,
Thou' all these years have passed.
And if one day our love rejoins,
Then my heart rejoice at last.

WORLD WAR II

Now fifty years have come to pass,
Since war it was declared.
And britain armed to cross the sea,
To free Europe from the enemy.

The war machine of Nazi Germany,
Tore across the land.
Enslaving other nations,
In the grip of Hitler's hands.

But in their way stood our small isle,
Who together with our friends.
Brought that mighty war machine,
To a justifiable end.

But sixty million lost their lives,
In that bloody six year war.
And we must always remember,
What those lives stand for.

For freedom is the right of man,
It is his right to choose.
And if for freedom man does fight,
Then he shall never ever lose.

BLINDED WORLD

It was the year of '39',
When we marched towards the Rhine.
To help our Polish allies,
Defeat the German line.

And for six long years the world did cry,
In anguish at her plight.
Until all men beneath her skies,
Were free from German might.

Young men died far on foreign lands,
No more to see their homes.
But they gave their lives for freedom,
What better was their cause.

So when you think of battle fields,
Remember in your minds.
That World War Two was fought for you,
And the freedom of mankind.

So join with soldiers young and old,
In remembrance of their kind.
Who fought a war for liberty,
When the world had become blind.

A MOTHERS BOY

The First World War was the war,
To end all other wars.
When men from foreign countries,
Died on foreign shores.
And when at last the Hun was beat,
Homeward sailed the fleet.

But lessons from that war,
Were lost in '39'.
And the countries of the world,
Fought another time.
And nation fought with nation,
Against a common foe.
And in the year of '45',
We dealt the final blow.

That war was fought for you and me,
And is etched within our history.
Now fifty years have passed us by,
And it's time the world remembered.
That 60 million lost their lives,
When the world one day she trembled.

So on the day of declaration,
The world recall as one great nation.
The generations of tomorrow,
Should not forget the debt.
That's owed to every soldier,
Who untied the Nazi net.

So stand together and bow your head,
In memory of your nations dead.
And lay a wreath by the Cenotaph,
To say thankyou on the worlds behalf.
For the freedom that you now enjoy,
Cost the life of a mother's boy.

OCEAN GRAVES

The sailor stands upon the deck,
The ocean battle over.
And of that mighty battle child,
Lies a burning metal wreck.

The ocean now awash with fire,
And screams of drowning men.
Are all that echoes from within,
An ocean funeral pyre.

But those brave men who died at sea,
Will never be forgot.
For they gave their lives for freedom,
In the fight for liberty.

And thou' they lie beneath the waves,
In their sunken battle tombs.
Their memory still lingers on,
From within their ocean graves.

And when wars anniversary,
Again comes round for them.
We must say a prayer,
To those warlords of the sea.

And cast your wreaths upon the waves,
In honour of your dead.
Who died while fighting tyranny,
And rest in ocean graves.

WINGED WARRIORS

The wings of death flew inbetween,
The pilots and the clouds.
And airmen flew with bated breath,
Awaiting for their shrouds.

A squadron full of warriors,
Within their metal birds.
Flew onwards into battle,
With freedom in their words.

Mosquitoes rained down from the night,
With guns ablaze they joined the fight.
And Spitfires spat out their fire,
While bombers lit the freedom pyre.

Above the clouds they flew,
At home within the sky.
Eyes searching for their enemy,
Not knowing when they'd die.

And far from home in hostile skies,
They flew their battle birds.
And listened to their comrades cries,
As death cut short their words.

So let your eyes remember skies,
That were once lit up by war.
And remember all those airmen,
Who died for freedoms cause.

LAND OF MAGIC

Elfs play games with fairie queens,
Unicorns dream magic dreams.
Warlocks cast their magic spells,
Dreamers pay the wishing wells.
Ogres hold their maidens fair,
While magic knights seek out their lair.
And time does not exist you see,
In this land of mystery.

Kings are throned on ocean waves,
In lands from far beyond the grave.
Tears of sadness never fall.
Behind the silver magic wall.
Witches fly across the sky,
Upon their magic broomsticks high.
And frogs turn into handsome prince's,
By a maiden's magic kisses.

This land of golden mystery,
Is not a land for you and me.
For we know war and we know hate,
And we may not pass through the gate.
But we may see this secret land,
At night within our dreams.
A passing glimpse of happiness,
Inside a ray of beams.

INSANITY

What's within my brain is dead,

Insanity of my head.

Futuristic killing spree,

Only way to set me free.

Insanity is what I see,

Future of my brain is none.

My only thoughts they are my own,

Why won't you leave my thoughts alone.

Crazy brain of insane man,

Thinking under summer sun.

Crazy thoughts of insanity,

What I say will be will be.

Fate is what the preacher said,

While sanity drowns within my head.

Insanity is what I see,

For my brain to be set free.

NEVER WASTE A CARE

The cold grey mists of dawn arise,
Unshackled from the night.
Chasing hidden shadows,
From the pathway of the light.

A burning light within the sky,
To free your soul and let you fly.
To rise above the chains of life,
You must cut them with the sacrificial knife.

Just live your life for what you are,
And do not chase a hidden star.
For life can be so full of fun,
So live it now before its run.

Do not wish what others have,
And never cry for more.
Just be happy always,
And never close your door.

And if one day your boat comes in,
Do not forget your friends.
And never rise above yourself,
Just because you have some new
Found wealth.

So when you wake each living day,
Just be glad your there.
And stand beneath a summers ray,
And never waste a care.

TURBULENT TIMES

He was just a young lad going off to the war,
He knew he was going and what to fight for.
He marched and he sang the songs of the men,
And walked into war to die where and when.

Now he's sitting in trenches all covered in mud,
While his mates are all dead all covered in blood.
The voices are silent no more do they sing,
But remember the horror of deaths dark icy sting.

The feelings are mutual on both of the sides,
Young men that are fighting for what they feel right.
All they remember is the taking of lives,
The taking of men from their children and wives.

And when it is over and all homeward bound,
They're leaving their comrades deep down in the ground.
And after the years deep down in their minds,
They'll remember the tears of their turbulent times.

SILENT EARTH

A solar flare a flash of light,
Then time it came to pass.
A blazing sun in a cold black sea,
In an endless sky of ebony.

A passing thought is etched within,
A billion years of time.
A future without sunshine,
In a world that's full of crime.

Three hundred years of peace we've had,
In three thousand years or more.
A planet always waring.
For a never ending cause.

But time will come one day for man,
And he'll fight his final war.
And the earth will spin in silence,
For our world will be no more.

FOREVER BE GLAD

Thoughts of the mind,
What do they mean.
At night in your dreams,
Can they be seen.
Visions of past lives,
And those yet to come.
Are thoughts found in dreamland,
From beyond a blue sun.

Dreams that have fallen,
And those yet to rise.
Are thoughts that are hidden,
Behind lost astral skies.
Visions to cherish,
And dreams yet to fear.
Are thoughts that are trapped,
In a lost golden tear.

Now remember these words,
That you have just read.
And dream of the future,
When nighttime to bed.
Don't fear what you dream for,
And never be sad.
Think thoughts for the future,
And forever be glad.

WALL

The war is over,

But just begun.

A city torn,

And on the run.

From east to west,

They start to flee.

Before a wall,

Ends the right to be free.

People who want,

To live in the west,

Are held by a wall,

And kept in the east.

Families divided,

But never to fall.

Look to each other,

From over the wall.

Watching a wall,

That divides their homeland.

Through years of oppression,

Their spirit still stands.

And as time passes by,

The old guard shall die,

And a call will cry out

For freedom.

THE FINAL ACT

There's no trees in the valleys,

And no grass on the ground.

No there's no trees in the valleys,

And the earth has no sound.

There's no people in the cities,

And no people in the towns.

There's no life anywhere,

Are they living underground.

Turning up the high street,

You see the bodies on the ground.

All the dead and the dying,

Lying there all around.

And as you run from the screaming,

You see a fire in the sky.

Another mushroom sprouting upwards,

And you wonder if you'll die.

The radiation deep inside you,

Begins to eat your soul away.

And now the final act begins,

Within this human play.

The earth begins at last to cry,

And now it heaves a final sigh.

And now it seems your going to die,

For putting fires in the sky.

SCOTLAND'S PEOPLE

Once we were free,
We could not be tamed.
And the people of Scotland,
Could never be shamed.
The Romans they tried,
But were lost in the mist,
Caught in the grip,
Of the great Scottish fist.

Our future was fought for,
By great highland men.
Who fought of the English,
In valley and glen.
But our future was lost,
By treacherous seeds.
Sown into some Scotsmen,
By foul English deeds.

But still we can win,
The freedom that's ours.
If all people in Scotland,
Fight back at the powers.
The powers that lie,
Deep south of our borders,
In a government of foreigners,
Who think they're our warders.